Intermediate Chinese

Learning Chinese with Science

中级汉语
中文科学园

Joy Betz and Chong An Chang

Cover image © Shutterstock Inc.

www.kendallhunt.com
Send all inquiries to:
4050 Westmark Drive
Dubuque, IA 52004-1840

Copyright © 2013 by Joy Betz and Chong An Chang

ISBN 978-1-4652-1520-8

Kendall Hunt Publishing Company has the exclusive rights to reproduce this work,
to prepare derivative works from this work, to publicly distribute this work,
to publicly perform this work and to publicly display this work.

All rights reserved. No part of this publication may be reproduced,
stored in a retrieval system, or transmitted, in any form or by any
means, electronic, mechanical, photocopying, recording, or otherwise,
without the prior written permission of the copyright owner.

Printed in the United States of America
10 9 8 7 6 5 4 3 2 1

Table of Contents

Preface
序

Lesson 1　　Heaven of Animals 1
第一课　　动物的天堂
Practical Chinese 1: Radicals
实用汉语　　偏旁

Lesson 2　　Story of Two Mothers 7
第二课　　两位妈妈的故事
Practical Chinese 2: Hobby
实用汉语　　爱好

Lesson 3　　Grow Taller and Taller ....…......13
第三课　　不停地长高
Practical Chinese 3: The use of "的、地、得"
实用汉语　　的、地、得的用法

Lesson 4　　A Debate on Sight 17
第四课　　关于眼光的争论
Practical Chinese 4: To visit an ophthalmologist
实用汉语　　看眼科医生

Lesson 5   Are Supersonic Cars Good? ………..23
第五课   超音速汽车好吗？
Practical Chinese 5: Vehicles (1)
实用汉语   汽车

Lesson 6   Free Travel Around the World ……....29
第六课   不花钱旅行世界
Practical Chinese 6: Vehicles (2)
实用汉语   汽车（续）

Lesson 7   You Be the Judge ……….....………..35
第七课   你来当法官
Practical Chinese 7: Weather
实用汉语   天气

Lesson 8   Three Ways of Heat Transfer ………..41
第八课   热传递的三种方式
Practical Chinese 8: Seasons/Festivals
实用汉语   季节/节日

Lesson 9   The "Slow Motion" …………...….…..47
第九课   走得慢的故事
Practical Chinese 9: University
实用汉语   大学

Lesson 10   True or False? ………………….….....53
第十课   大实话
Practical Chinese 10: Temperatures and more
实用汉语   知识：温度及其它

Lesson 11　　Rules to Make a Turn ……………….....59
第十一课　　转弯的学问
Practical Chinese 11: Getting Directions
实用汉语　　指路

Lesson 12　　Go Ahead of Time ……………..…….…65
第十二课　　走在时间的前面
Practical Chinese 12: Friends
实用汉语　　朋友

Lesson 13　　Story of the Sun and the Cold Wind…71
第十三课　　太阳和秋风的故事
Practical Chinese 13: Party
实用汉语　　晚会

Lesson 14　　Monk Tang Crossed a River ………..…77
第十四课　　唐僧过河
Practical Chinese 14: Travel
实用汉语　　旅行

Lesson 15　　Are Scientists Wrong? ……..……..….85
第十五课　　科学家错了吗？
Practical Chinese 15: Dreams (1)
实用汉语　　理想（一）

Lesson 16　　Confucius and Two Kids ……..……...91
第十六课　　孔子和两个小儿的故事
Practical Chinese 16: Dreams (2)
实用汉语　　理想（二）

Preface

This book, ***Intermediate Chinese --- Learning Chinese with Science***, is the second book in a series written for North American learners who wish to study the Chinese language and literature. The book contains 16 lessons and uses short scientific stories to help learners readily grasp the meaning of the language as well as appreciate the nuances in its applications.

Although various Chinese textbooks are available on the market today, most of them are designed for beginners. Entry level textbooks usually pay attention to the practical aspects such as how to communicate in an airport, at a bus stop, in a store, or in a restaurant. These books are useful and practical, but readers may not be able to move beyond the technical aspects to enjoy the beauty of the language and develop an understanding for the literature.

Our books are themselves good articles worth reading. We focus on generating reader interest and linking language skills with advanced grammar, and literary application such as idioms. Learners can progress at a steady and continuous pace by following the lessons contained in this and the other books in our series: *Essential Chinese --- Learning Chinese with Fun; Intermediate Chinese --- Learning Chinese with Science;* and *Advanced Chinese --- Understanding China*.

In this series, each lesson has a list of words, questions, and exercises. Every lesson contains two parts: the *Main Text* and the *Practical Chinese*. The practical part is designed to help the students handle situations such as "greetings", "shopping", "at a party", and get used to oral communications. If the learner still needs basic training in speaking Chinese, he/she can bypass the *Main Text* and concentrate on the *Practical Chinese* first. If basic Chinese (greetings, etc.) is already mastered, concentrating on the *Main Text* will help them enjoy the rich contents of this book fully.

This offers flexibility for learners at all levels and enables the teaching professional to take a more personalized, learner-based approach.

In this book Lesson 13 is a well-known fable. Lesson 16 originates from one story in the ancient Chinese philosophy book *Lie Zi* (written between 450 B.C and 375 B.C). Other 14 lessons were written by the authors of this book. We, the authors have both received formal training in Science and in Chinese language, and have extensive experience in teaching courses in USA and Canada. These books are suitable for Chinese courses at various levels offered in North America. We welcome input and feedback from readers in order to make continued improvements.

Joy Betz (USA)
Chong An Chang (Canada)

序

　　这本中文教材**中级汉语 --- 中文科学园**，是给在北美的汉语学习者编写的，一共16课，风格生动有趣，由许多和科学有关的幽默小故事组成，启发智慧让人更为聪明。全书课文逐步加深自成体系，内涵丰富，教师可以选择使用。

　　虽然现在有各种汉语教材问世，但是多数都是入门程度，注重实用，教读者在不同的场合（见面、机场、银行、商店、旅行、餐馆、家庭等等）该怎么说话的基本教材，内容多是"你好"、"请问"、"我是…"等等的基本口语训练。这些课本相当实用，但是文学性不强。读者还不能从中欣赏中文的美好。

　　这本汉语书注意课文的文学性。我们的整套教材包含三本书，第一本**基础汉语---中文益智宫**强调幽默易懂的风格。这一本**中级汉语 --- 中文科学园**把课文和生物、物理等自然科学相结合。第三本**高级汉语 --- 了解中国**文字优美，每一课都是很好的中文文学教材，还包括了大量的历史、文学、语言、人文地理、旅游知识。全套书越往后有越多的成语出现，能提高学生的读写和欣赏水平。全书引导学生学习更多的汉字、更多的成语，喜欢汉语、了解中国、热爱中国语言和中国文学。

　　本书每一课都有词汇表、成语讲解、问题讨论和作业练习。每课后面都专门写了"实用汉语"。这些实用汉语正是针对汉语基础、听力和口语还不够好的读者对"问候"、"商店"、"旅行"等实用场合口语的训练。所以，如果你感觉程度还不够，不妨"喧宾夺主"，先放开主课文，着重每课的

"实用汉语"部分，集中补课加强对实用汉语的学习。如果你已经学会了各种实用场合的口语，请你集中精力到主课，欣赏每一课的主课文和课文的解释，提高水平更上一层楼，熟悉中国的历史和文学，学会汉语这门古老而有用的学问。

本书第 13 课太阳和秋风的故事是民间广泛流传的寓言，第16课孔子和两个小儿的故事源自中国古代文献《列子·汤问》篇，其余的 14 课是由本书作者创作的。本书的两位作者既在中国受过严格的文科和理科教育，又在美国、加拿大从事教学实践多年。这套教材适用于美国和加拿大汉语作为第二语言的课堂教学，欢迎使用者提出宝贵建议。

看五洲四海，学习中文的浪潮云水翻腾风雷激荡，越来越多的人认识到，汉语不仅仅是一门有悠久历史的古老语言，而且是当今世界各国经济交流和文化来往必不可少的重要语言工具。在西方世界普及汉语教育，此其时也。愿大家携手共进，把汉语教育的浪潮推向新的高度。

Joy Betz （美国）
常崇安 （加拿大）

Lesson 1
Heaven of Animals
第一课　动物的天堂

　　平平看到在新建的动物园里，梅花鹿在悠闲地迈步、大象在休息、鸟儿在歌唱、许多美丽的天鹅在池子里游来游去，大家和平相处，一片悠悠然的景象。他高兴地对妈妈说：现在的动物园真是动物的天堂，动物们在这里不愁吃不愁生病，饿了有管理员哥哥姐姐来喂食，病了有兽医专家来打针治病。多好啊！

　　可是妈妈却说：你为动物们着想很好，但是你说得不全对，住在动物园里对动物们并不太有利。动物也是需要自由的，在大自然中它们与危险搏斗，在大风大浪中成长，比在温室里更健康。

　　平平明白了妈妈的意思，学到了这个道理。

词汇 Words

新建	xīn jiàn	new built
梅花鹿	méi huā lù	deer
悠闲	yōu xián	relax
悠悠然	yōu yōu rán	leisurely
大象	dà xiàng	elephant
天鹅	tiān é	swan
天堂	tiān táng	Heaven
管理员	guǎn lǐ yuán	care taking person
兽医	shòu yī	veterinarian
打针	dǎ zhēn	shot a needle, injection
治病	zhì bìng	cure
危险	wēi xiǎn	danger
搏斗	bó dòu	fight
温室	wēn shì	hothouse

成语 Idiom
大风大浪　　dà fēng dà làng　storm, big upheaval

问题 Question
为什么妈妈说动物园并不是动物理想的天堂？
Mom says that the zoo is not an ideal place for animals, why not?

练习 Exercises
[1] 请你用"悠悠然"造一个句。
Construct a sentence using the word "悠悠然"。
[2] 用中文写 1 篇和动物有关的短文。
Write a short article in Chinese about animals.

实用汉语 Practical Chinese (1)
偏旁 Radicals

A 什么是偏旁？ What are radicals?

偏旁很有用。汉语里有很多字由两部分组成的，左边右边或者上边下边。例如骑、驰、驴、驼等都有"马"部，这些字都和马有某种关联。又如吃、喝、叫、吵等都是"口"部的字，都和"口"意义相关。学会了偏旁，学习汉语（读、写）就方便得多。

Radicals are useful. Many Chinese characters are made of two parts. For example 骑(ride), 驰(galloping)、驴(donkey)、驼(camel) etc.; all of them have some kind of relation with the animal horse ("马" in Chinese). The radical of these characters therefore is "马". Words like 吃(eat), 喝(drink), 叫(shout), 吵(quarrel) all have a common radical of "口" (the mouth). It is much easier to remember Chinese words if you learn their structure and their radicals first.

B 指出下列汉字的偏旁
Point out the radical of the following characters

[1] 烧、烤、炼   (burn, roast, temper with fire)
[2] 鸡、鸭、鹅   (chicken, duck, goose)
[3] 狗、狐、狼   (dog, fox, wolf)
[4] 树、林、椅   (tree, forest, chair)
[5] 河、洋、海   (river, ocean, sea)

C 把相同偏旁的字挑出来放在一起
Place characters with the same radical together.

蛇	shé	snake	他	tā	him	
冻	dòng	freeze	姨	yí	mom's sister	
疮	chuāng	skin ulcer	蛆	qū	maggot	
病	bìng	ill, sick	坝	bà	dam	
晴	qíng	fine (weather)	你	nǐ	you	
冰	bīng	ice	痛	tòng	hurt, pain	
地	dì	ground	蜈蚣	wú gōng	centipede	
妈	mā	mother	明	míng	bright	
妹	mèi	younger sister	冷	lěng	cold	
蜂	fēng	bee	伯	bó	uncle	
坎	kǎn	ridge	昨	zuó	yesterday	

Lesson 2
Story of Two Mothers
第二课 两位妈妈的故事

蝴蝶妈妈是昆虫世界最漂亮的女士，她那美丽的双翅，在万花丛中飞扬起伏，把春意带给人间。青蛙妈妈是捉害虫的模范，每天忙忙碌碌，是人类的好朋友。可是她们一个在天上飞不会游泳，一个住在小河沟里不会上天。有一天，她们交谈起来，发现她们原来有着共同的地方。

原来，蝴蝶妈妈的孩子是毛毛虫，青蛙妈妈的孩子是小蝌蚪，她们的子女都长得和自己完全不一样！

词汇 Words

蝴蝶	hú dié	butterfly
昆虫	kūn chóng	insect
漂亮	piào liàng	pretty
美丽	měi lì	beautiful
双翅	shuāng chì	two wings
春意	chūn yì	smell of spring
飞扬起伏	fēi yáng qǐ fú	fly up and down
青蛙	qīng wā	frog

害虫	hài chóng	pests
游泳	yóu yǒng	swim
模范	mó fàn	model, example
河沟	hé gōu	brook
交谈	jiāo tán	talk, conversation
发现	fā xiàn	discover
毛毛虫	máo máo chóng	caterpillars
蝌蚪	kē dǒu	tadpoles

成语 Idioms

万花丛中	wàn huā chóng zhōng among million flowers
忙忙碌碌	máng máng lù lù busy, rush

问题 Questions

[1] 蝴蝶妈妈和青蛙妈妈有哪些不同？
What are the differences between mom butterfly and mom frog?

[2] 她们又有什么共同的地方？
What do they have in common?

练习 Exercises

[1] 在网上学习有关蝌蚪和毛虫的知识，懂得它们是怎么变化成青蛙和蝴蝶的。
Learn about tadpoles and caterpillars. Understand how they evolve into frogs and butterflies.

[2] 想出一个AABB（就像"忙忙碌碌"）结构的成语例子。
Give an example of an idiom that has the structure AABB, like the idiom "忙忙碌碌" in this text.

实用汉语 Practical Chinese (2)
爱好 Hobby

A. 词汇 Words

下棋	xià qí	play chess
唱歌	chàng gē	singing songs
画画	huà huà	drawing, painting
书法	shū fǎ	calligraphy
锻炼	duàn liàn	physical excrise
钓鱼	diào yú	fishing
做饭	zuò fàn	cooking
游山玩水	yóu shān wán shuǐ	sightseeing tour
木工	mù gōng	carpenter
开汽车	kāi qì chē	driving
聊天	liáo tiān	chat
写小说	xiě xiǎo shuō	write a novel
休闲	xiū xián	relax

B. 对话 Dialogue

你平时都爱好些什么呀？
Nǐ píng shí dōu ài hào xiē shé mō ya?
What hobby do you have?

我爱好唱歌和锻炼身体。
Wǒ ài hào chàng gē hé duàn liàn shēn tǐ.
I like singing and exercising.

我也爱好唱歌，但是我同时也爱好钓鱼和做饭。
Wǒ yě ài hào chàng gē, dàn shì wǒ tóng shí yě ài hào diào yú hé zuò fàn.
I like singing too, however I also like fishing and cooking.

有些人爱好游山玩水，开汽车。我喜欢在家静静地写小说。
Yǒu xiē rén ài hào yóu shān wán shuǐ, kāi qì chē. Wǒ xǐ huān zài jiā jìng jìng dì xiě xiǎo shuō.
Some people love sightseeing tours and driving. I like to write novels quietly at home.

写小说很有意思啊，不过我更喜欢做木工，锻炼身体。
Xiě xiǎo shuō hěn yǒu yì sī à, bú guò wǒ gèng xǐ huān zuò mù gōng, duàn liàn shēn tǐ.
It would be interesting to write a novel. However, for me, I like woodworking and exercising.

小王是下棋的高手，琳达喜欢中国书法和画画。
Xiǎo wáng shì xià qí de gāo shǒu, lín dá xǐ huān zhōng guó shū fǎ hé huà huà.
Xiao Wang can play chess well, while Linda loves Chinese calligraphy and painting.

和人聊天不错，也是一种休闲。
Hé rén liáo tiān bú cuò, yě shì yī zhǒng xiū xián.
It is good to chat with people. That is a kind of relaxation too.

C. 汉译英
Translate the following into English

[1] 妈妈喜欢写书，爸爸爱好钓鱼。
[2] 我不爱好钓鱼，我爱好书法。
[3] 约翰很喜欢画画，他画得不错。
[4] 安德森的最大的爱好是做饭，他做的菜很好吃 (delicious)。
[5] 老李喜欢游山玩水，她走了很多地方。

D. 英译汉
Translate the following into Chinese

[1] Jeff（杰夫）has a hobby. He loves travel.

[2] Xiao Zhang likes many activities（活动）. She likes painting, writing and calligraphy.

[3] My grandfather is a good carpenter, he made many good things.

[4] My sister likes sightseeing tours, she does not like sports.

[5] Mary, how do you spend your time when you just want to relax?

Lesson 3
Grow Taller and Taller
第三课 不停地长高

爸爸说，小孩子是在不停地长高的。埃米不同意。她说：老师告诉我们，每个人在早上比在当天晚上要高，平躺着睡了一觉，人的骨骼放松了，第二天早上人就会高一些。站了一天，压了一天，人就会变得稍微矮一点。小朋友们就是这样螺旋形地长高、变矮、再长高的。

爸爸不知道这对不对，埃米就真的做了实验。连续几天测量的结果，果然人在早上要更高一点。看到实验的结果，爸爸笑了，表扬了可爱的小埃米。

词汇 Words

平躺	píng tǎng	lie down flat
骨骼	gǔ gé	skeleton
放松	fàng sōng	relax
稍微	shāo wēi	slightly
矮	ǎi	short
螺旋形	luó xuán xíng	spiral
实验	shí yàn	experiment
测量	cè liáng	measure

| 表扬 | biǎo yáng | praise |
| 结果 | jié guǒ | result |

问题 Questions

[1] 为什么埃米要连续做几天的测量实验？只做 1 天不好吗？

Why did Amy do the measurement for several days instead of doing it only once? What is the advantage of repeating an experiment?

[2] 为什么人在早上比晚间高一点？什么叫做"螺旋形地长高"？

Why is a person a little bit taller in the morning than in the evening? What does "growing up in spiral form" mean to you?

练习 Exercise

遇到问题亲自动手做实验找出答案。这种学习方法值得我们学习。自选一个题目设计一个简单可行的实验去证明一个说法是对或者不对。

It is a good idea to design an experiment and do it to prove or disprove a hypothesis. Please choose a topic by yourself, then design and discuss your experiment.

实用汉语 Practical Chinese (3)
"的、地、得"的用法
The use of "的、地、得"

"的"用于形容词或代词，形容"的"字之后的名词，例如"美丽的姑娘"、"幸福的生活"、"她的书包"。

"地"用于副词，修饰在"地"字之后的动词，例如"很快地走来"、"伤心地哭"。

"得"是形容"得"字之前的动作，例如"哭得很伤心"、"走得快"。

练习 Exercise

本课的课文里有"不停地长高"、"人的骨骼"、"变得稍微矮一点"、"螺旋形地长高"、"测量的结果"、"实验的结果"、"可爱的小埃米"等说法，请你根据上面的理论研究这些句子里"的"、"地"、"得"的不同用法。

改错 Correct the mistakes when using "的"、"地"、"得"

[1] 老师讲的很快，我没有听懂。

[2] 妈妈慢慢得抬起头，望着我。

[3] 勤快地阿婆每天很早就起来。

［4］我把那件事很快得忘了。

［5］忘记不愉快地事是很难的，人会记地很牢地

［6］最好得方法就是设计一个实验。

［7］美丽地姑娘千千万，只有你最可爱。

［8］他得家很幸福，每天他都起的很早努力的工作。

［9］妈妈地朋友小王得名字很好听。

［10］她把车开地更快了，她得朋友害怕的很。

Lesson 4
A Debate on Sight
第四课 关于眼光的争论

从前曾经有过一场关于眼光的争论。

一些人说：我们能够看到东西，是因为我们的眼里往外射出"眼光"，眼光落在哪里我们就看见那里的东西。如果把眼闭上，眼光射不出去，就什么也看不到了。把头扭到一侧，我们的眼光就会射向那一侧，而看不到原来的一侧。把眼睁大，射出的眼光就多，看得就更清楚。我们常说，某人眼光锐利、眼光不凡、很有眼光等等，不是吗？

也有人不同意。他们认为，眼是不会发出光的。我们能看到事物，是因为有光线射到我们的眼中。如果把眼闭上了，光就射不进来了。

你认为哪一种说法对呢？用什么事实或者实验可以证明另外那一种说法不正确呢？

词汇 Words

眼光	yǎn guāng	sight
闭上	bì shàng	close
扭	niǔ	turn, twist
一侧	yī cè	one side
锐利	ruì lì	sharp
事实	shì shí	fact
实验	shí yàn	experiment
证明	zhèng míng	prove, proof

练习 Exercises

[1] 和同学们讨论，哪一种说法对？怎样设计一个实验去加以证明？

Discuss with the class which theory is correct. How can you design an experiment to prove that one theory is correct and the other theory is wrong?

[2] 课文里的"眼光锐利"、"眼光不凡"、"很有眼光"，都不完全是在说眼睛，而是含"见识"在内。用"眼光"的这种意思造句。

Construct a sentence using the word "眼光" (which can also mean knowledge, insight).

实用汉语 Practical Chinese (4)
看眼科医生
To visit an ophthalmologist

A 词汇 Words

眼科	yǎn kē	ophthalmology
医院	yī yuàn	hospital
护士	hù shì	nurse
手术	shǒu shù	operation, surgery
安静	ān jìng	quiet
医生	yī shēng	doctor
院长	yuàn zhǎng	director
麻醉	má zuì	anesthesia
恢复	huī fú	recover
痛	tòng	painful, ache, hurt
白内障	bái nèi zhàng	cataract
肾脏	shèn zàng	kidney
门诊	mén zhěn	out patient
眼药	yǎn yào	eye drop
健康	jiàn kāng	healthy

B 用汉语和英语念下面的对话
Read the dialogue in both Chinese and English

------ 护士,我可以见眼科的肯尼迪医生吗?
Hù shì, wǒ kě yǐ jiàn yǎn kē de kěn ní dí yī shēng mā?
Nurse, may I see Dr. Kennedy of the ophthalmology department?

------ 请先休息,她马上就来。
Qǐng xiān xiū xí, tā mǎ shàng jiù lái
Please have a seat, she will be here soon.

------ 肯尼迪医生,您看我的眼有什么问题呢?
Kěn ní dí yī shēng, nín kàn wǒ de yǎn yǒu shé mō wèn tí ne?
Dr. Kennedy, what do you think about my eyes, anything wrong?

------ 你有白内障,需要动手术。
Nǐ yǒu bái nèi zhàng, xū yào dòng shǒu shù.
You have cataracts. You need a surgery.

------ 手术会痛吗?
Shǒu shù huì tòng mā?
Will the operation be painful?

------ 不痛。会有麻醉的,手术后恢复一星期,继续用药一个月就行了。
Bú tòng. huì yǒu má zuì dé, shǒu shù hòu huī fú yī xīng qī, jì xù yòng yào yī gè yuè jiù xíng le.

It doesn't hurt. There will be anesthesia. You will recover within one week following the surgery. Use medicine for one more month and it's done.

------ 但是我肾脏不大好，服药有问题吗？
Dàn shì wǒ shèn zàng bú dà hǎo, fú yào yǒu wèn tí ma?
However I know my kidney has some problems, can I take the medicine?

------ 没问题，你放心好了。是滴眼药。手术就在门诊进行不住院。
Méi wèn tí, nǐ fàng xīn hǎo le. shì dī yǎn yào. Shǒu shù jiù zài mén zhěn jìn xíng bú zhù yuàn.
Don't worry, the medication will be eye-drops only. You don't need to stay in hospital.

------ 我的视力能恢复吗？
Wǒ de shì lì néng huī fú ma?
Can my vision get back to normal after the surgery?

------ 不但能，而且你的眼会比原来更健康的。
Bú dàn néng, ér qiě nǐ dé yǎn huì bǐ yuán lái gèng jiàn kāng de.
Sure, not only that, your vision will be better than before.

------ 谢谢您！
Xiè xiè nín!
Thank you!

C 把下列词组或者句子译为汉语
Translate the following into Chinese

[1] left eye, right eye
[2] cataract surgery
[3] You will need three types of eye drops after the surgery.
[4] Start to use eye drop # 1 three days before the operation.
[5] Your vision will reach 20/20 in the future.
[6] The operation is free to you, you don't need to pay.
[7] Eat normally, don't worry too much, it is only a small operation.
[8] Your appointment is 8 AM next Wednesday.
[9] Dr. Kennedy is an excellent doctor. She has done this kind of surgery 5000 times (五千次).
[10] Do not swim, do not rub (摩擦) your eyes for at least one month after the surgery.

Lesson 5
Are Supersonic Cars Good?
第五课 超音速汽车好吗？

我们生活在一个高速的时代。整个社会都在"提速"，人们更忙了，社会发展的步伐越来越快。

那么，让我们的汽车公司把新汽车设计成超音速的岂不是更好？开这样的车才过瘾。油门一踩，流线型的汽车跑得比声音还快。

但是，工程师阿姨却说了：不行。那样不仅没法在红灯面前停下来，而且对前边的行人也是极大的威胁。因为汽车发出的声音比车走得还慢，人在被撞上前根本无知无觉，一点儿声音也听不见。这种无声无息的车要开过去一会儿，声音才传到。那将是多么大的灾难啊！

词汇 Words

高速	gāo sù	high speed
社会	shè huì	society
提速	tí sù	increase the speed
发展	fā zhǎn	develop
步伐	bù fá	step
设计	shè jì	design
超音速	chāo yīn sù	supersonic
过瘾	guò yǐn	fun
油门	yóu mén	gas pedal
流线型	liú xiàn xíng	streamline
工程师	gōng chéng shī	engineer
威胁	wēi xié	threaten
声音	shēng yīn	sound
灾难	zāi nàn	disaster

成语 Idioms

无知无觉　　wú zhī wú jué
　　　　　　without knowing, unconscious
无声无息　　wú shēng wú xí
　　　　　　without sound

问题 Questions

[1] 为什么汽车不是越快越好？
The fastest car is not necessarily the best car, why not?
[2] 为什么人们不能先听到后面传来的超音速汽车的声音？
Why can people not hear supersonic cars coming from behind?

练习 Exercises

[1] 在网上学习有关超音速飞机的知识。
Read about supersonic airplanes from the internet.

[2] 用"无声无息"造句。
Construct a sentence using the idiom "无声无息".

[3] 你梦想里的现代飞机像什么样？画 1 张图，在图中画出你心目中最现代化的飞机的样子。
Draw your dream airplane on a piece of paper. What does it look like?

实用汉语 Practical Chinese (5)
汽车 Vehicles (1)

A. 词汇 Words

汽车	qì chē	car
卡车	kǎ chē	truck
救护车	jiù hù chē	ambulance
救火车	jiù huǒ chē	fire truck
摩托车	mō tuō chē	motorcycle
油电混合车	qì diàn hùn hé chē	hybrid car
巴士	bā shì	bus
公共	gōng gòng	public
面包车	miàn bāo chē	van
小客车	xiǎo kè chē	van
出租车	chū zū chē	taxi
穿梭小巴	chuān suō xiǎo bā	shuttle
机场	jī chǎng	airport
旅馆	lǚ guǎn	hotel
灰狗巴士	hūi góu bā shì	The Greyhound Bus
油罐车	yóu guàn chē	tanker
越野车	yuè yě chē	SUV
摩托车	mō tuō chē	motorcycle

B. 课文 Text

马路上跑着很多汽车。有送油的油罐车、运货的大卡车；有许多巴士（公共汽车），最出名的就是灰狗巴士；还有出租车和在飞机场和旅馆之间的穿梭小巴。家家户户都有自己的小汽车、越野车、面包车、甚至还有摩托车。还有的人开爱护环境 (eco-friendly) 的油电混合车。汽车给人们带来了生活的方便。所有的车辆都要给救火车和救护车让路，因为它们是去救人的。

**C.
把上面的课文译为英语
Translate the above paragraph into English.**

Lesson 6
Free Travel Around the World
第六课 不花钱旅行世界

　　小雅坐在院子里望向天空，非常专心，好久一动也不动。她在看蓝天，想飞行的事。她想，咱们的地球不是在不停地自转吗？我们可以设计一个大气球，带我们升入高空。这样我们就能看见地球在脚下转啊转。一会儿昆仑山、喜玛拉雅山转过来了，一会儿中东和非洲转过来了，一会儿美洲转过来了。等到迪斯尼世界乐园转来的时候，我们就把气球里的气放掉，气球就会慢慢地自己降落在地面。那样不是就可以到美国的迪斯尼世界去玩了吗？玩够了以后还可以用同样的办法回家。不用让爸爸妈妈给我们买飞机票，就可以到全世界任何一个地方去玩了。

　　请你想一想，小雅可以用这种方法免费旅游全球吗？

Disney World, Florida, USA 迪斯尼世界

词汇 Words

专心	zhuān xīn	concentrate
蓝天	lán tiān	blue sky
地球	dì qiú	Earth
自转	zì zhuǎn	rotation
设计	shè jì	design
气球	qì qiú	balloon
中东	zhōng dōng	Middle East
非洲	fēi zhōu	Africa
美洲	měi zhōu	America
降落	jiàng luò	landing
免费	miǎn fèi	free
旅游	lǚ yóu	travel

昆仑山	kūn lún shān The Kun Lun Mountains
喜马拉雅山	xǐ mǎ lā yǎ shān The Himalayas Mountains

迪斯尼世界　　　dí sī ní shì jiè
　　　　　　　　Disney World

问题 Questions

[1] 小雅的办法可以行得通吗，为什么？
What do you think about Xiao Ya's plan, why?
[2] 气球为什么能够升空？
How can a balloon rise to the sky?

练习 Exercise

用中文写一封给小雅的信，鼓励她的独立思考精神，并告诉她为什么那个办法不行。

Write a letter to Xiao Ya in Chinese, encourage her to continue thinking and explain to her why her plan shall not work.

实用汉语 Practical Chinese (6)
汽车 Vehicles (2)

A. 词汇 Words

引擎	yǐn qíng	engine
车轮	chē lún	wheel
方向盘	fāng xiàng pán	steering wheel
刹车	shā chē	brake
工具箱	gōng jù xiāng	tool box
行李箱	xíng lǐ xiāng	trunk
赛车	sài chē	racing car
老车	lǎo chē	very old car
贵	guì	expensive
便宜	pián yí	cheap
距离	jù lí	distance
速度	sù dù	speed
燃料	rán liào	fuel
价格	jià gé	price
耗油量	hào yóu liàng	fuel consumption
汽油	qì yóu	gasoline (gas)
柴油	chái yóu	diesel
汽车博览会	qì chē bó lǎn huì	Car Expo
概念车	gài niàn chē	concept car
下一代	xià yī dài	next generation
发展	fā zhǎn	development
趋势	qū shì	trend
宝马	bǎo mǎ	BMW
丰田	fēng tián	Toyota
福特	fú tè	Ford

B. 课文 Text

一辆汽车有一个引擎、4 个或更多的车轮。方向盘很重要，使我们可以掌握方向。刹车也同样重要，使我们可以停车。许多人把一个工具箱放在车的行李箱里。车用了几年就便宜了，但是很老的车反而很贵。什么样的车是好车呢？如果车跑同样的距离而耗油量少，就是好车。好车的价格可能并不贵，赛车是很贵的因为它们能跑出非常高的速度。

汽车有用汽油作燃料的，有用柴油作燃料的，还有油电混合车。世界上有各种牌子的汽车。如果你到汽车博览会参观，还可以看到五花八门的各种概念车，它们代表了下一代汽车的发展新趋势

C. 汉译英和英译汉

Translate English into Chinese and Chinese into English.

[1] 约翰有 1 辆油电混合的丰田车。

[2] 马丁先生很爱他的红色福特车。

[3] 这辆白色的汽车比那辆蓝色的汽车更贵一些。

[4] 引擎不好的汽车不是好车，刹车不好的汽车更不能开，很危险。

[5] 妈妈开的宝马车的引擎很好，爸爸开的越野车的刹车很好。

[6] How much is this BMW? It is not cheap.

[7] A good car runs fast and consumes less fuel. Hybrid cars are good cars.

[8] In general cars become less expensive when they become older; however those "ancient" cars are really expensive.

[9] A car may run faster than a train, but a high speed train usually runs faster than a car.

[10] May I see your SUV? I like SUV and trucks. I don't like small cars.

[11] I love Ford cars. They are beautiful.

[12] Toyota cars are Japanese cars. Japanese cars maybe and may not be Toyota cars.

[13] Some Japanese cars are made in other countries.

[14] I like hybrid cars, they use less gas.

[15] This BMW is not cheap, but it is beautiful. I love it.

Lesson 7
You Be the Judge
第七课 你来当法官

老师讲牛顿第三定律，说当甲给乙一个作用力的时候，乙也同时给甲一个反方向的同样大小的力。

如果有一个坏人打了一个人，在法庭上坏人引用牛顿第三定律说，当我打他的时候他也在打我，不折不扣地用了同样大小的力，时间也一秒也不少。所以要么两个人同样有罪，要么同时无罪。

老师让大家自己来当一回法官，看看怎么才能驳斥那个坏人似是而非的言论。

珍妮说：虽然牛顿定律是真理，但是如果看击中的前一瞬间就知道因果关系。谁是在运动（出击），谁是在不动（挨打）的。哪一方主动很清楚。

尼尔说：虽然作用力和反作用力是一样大的，但是效果完全可以不同。一拳可以打坏别人的身体，但反作用力不过是作用在打人的那拳头上，疼痛和后果完全不同。

老师说珍妮和尼尔说得好，科学定律是不可能用来为犯罪行为辩护的。

词汇 Words

作用力	zuò yòng lì	action
反作用力	fǎn zuò yòng lì	reaction
法庭	fǎ tíng	Court
有罪	yǒu zuì	guilty
无罪	wú zuì	not guilty
犯罪	fàn zuì	commit a crime
驳斥	bó chì	denounce, refute
真理	zhēn lǐ	truth
一瞬间	yī shùn jiān	one instant
因果关系	yīn guǒ guān xì	causality
效果	xiào guǒ	effect
拳头	quán tóu	fist
辩护	biàn hù	defend
牛顿第三定律	Niú Dùn dì sān dìng lǜ	Newton's third law

成语 Idioms

不折不扣　　bù zhé bù kòu　　　absolutely, hundred percent
似是而非　　sì shì ér fēi　　　sounds true, but actually not

问题 Questions

[1] 那位犯罪嫌疑人有权替自己辩护。他的辩护从表面看是很讲科学的，这样对他有什么好处？
The suspect had the right to defend himself. His argument seemed to be scientific. Why did he want to quote the famous Newton's third law?

[2] 为什么法官没有接受那人的辩护呢？
Why did the Judge not accept the defence of the suspect?

练习 Exercises

[1] 假设你是法官应该怎么讲？写 1 篇法官的讲演辞。
Assume you are the Judge; write a verdict for this case.

[2] 你一定学习过牛顿的第一、第二定律，用英文和中文表述之。
You must have learned Newton's First Law and Second Law. Write them in English first, then in Chinese.

实用汉语 Practical Chinese (7)
天气 Weather

A 词汇 Words

温度	wēn dù	temperature
下雪	xià xué	snow
雨	yǔ	rain
寒冷	hán lěng	cold
凉爽	liáng shuǎng	cool
热	rè	hot
温暖	wēn nuǎn	warm
气候	qì hòu	climate
预报	yù bào	forecasting
趋向	qū xiàng	trend, tendency
准确	zhǔn què	accurate
误差	wù chā	error
伞	sǎn	umbrella
太阳帽	tài yáng mào	sun hat
地震	dì zhèn	earthquake
长期	cháng qī	long term
短期	duǎn qī	short term
卫星	wèi xīng	satellite
越来越冷	yuè lái yuè lěng	colder and colder
小心	xiǎo xīn	careful
预计	yù jì	predict
回顾	huí gù	recall

B 英译汉
Translate the following sentences into Chinese

[1] The weather is getting colder and colder
[2] It is warm today, but it will not be as warm tomorrow.
[3] It is easy to forecast tomorrow's weather, but hard to predict an earthquake for the next week.
[4] It is relatively（相对）easy to predict the trend of earthquakes in the next century（世纪）; but it is hard to forecast weather for the next century.
[5] In winter the weather is cold, sometimes it snows.
[6] In summer the weather is hot. We swim on hot summer days.
[7] When we watch weather forecasting, be careful. The predictions may not be accurate.
[8] Umbrellas are useful on rainy days. Hats are helpful in hot weather.
[9] Every weather forecast may contain an error, either big or small
[10] Tom, I want to know the weather for tomorrow. Do you know it?

C 汉译英
Translate the following sentences into English.

[1] 这个月有很多晴天，下雨天很少。
[2] 明儿的天气怎样？
[3] 地震预报比天气预报更难。
[4] 我不知道下个月的天气会怎样，但我知道冬天已经不远了。
[5] 丽莎喜欢夏天，茱莉喜欢冬天。
[6] 没有一个地方的天气预报是永远完全准确的。

[7] 天有不测风云，记住带上你的雨伞。
[8] 不看天气预报的电视就开车出远门是不好的。
[9] 我们喜欢好天气。我们不喜欢不好的天气。
[10] 请问，下星期的天气好吗？可以去旅行吗？

Snow!
下雪啦

Lesson 8
Three Ways of Heat Transfer
第八课 热传递的三种方式

热传递的三种方式传导、对流和辐射，可以用篮球场上的传球来比喻。传导就像队员们一个个站着不移动，只是把球从一个人手上递给下一个人。如果这条线断了，球就传不过去。有的队传得快，是"良导体"，有的队传得极慢，是"绝缘体"。

第二种方式是对流。假设球场两头各有一队队员，这头的队员每人抱了一个篮球，那边的队员空手或者抱了很小的小皮球。一声令下大家都往对面飞跑，篮球就很快地从球场一头传到另一头去了。这种方式传递是很有效的。这就是对流。

第三种方式是辐射。队员把球直接扔向另一边，中间不需要任何"媒质"传递。就像太阳光把热量直接越过真空辐射到四面八方、也辐射到地球上一样。我们的世界依赖太阳的辐射，才有了温暖、有了光和热、有了万千气象。

词汇 Words

热传递	rè chuán dì	heat transfer
传导	chuán dào	heat conduction
对流	duì liú	convection
辐射	fú shè	radiation
比喻	bǐ yù	analogy
媒质	méi zhì	medium
良导体	liáng dào tǐ	good conductor
绝缘体	jué yuán tǐ	insulator
真空	zhēn kōng	vacuum

成语 Idioms

四面八方	sì miàn bā fāng	all directions
万千气象	wàn qiān qì xiàng	all scenes

讲解 Explanation

这一课老师没有直接讲物理学，而是用比喻，以形象的文例来说明。这样的讲法有什么好处？

The teacher did not talk about the physics nature of heat transfer, instead she explained the three ways using analogy. What is the advantage of this method of teaching?

实用汉语 Practical Chinese (8)
季节/节日 Seasons/Festivals

A 词汇 Words

春、夏、秋、冬
cūn, xià, qiū, dōng
spring, summer, fall (autumn), winter

旱季、雨季
hàn jì, yǔ jì
the dry season, the rainy season

庆祝
qìng zhú
celebrate (celebration)

元旦
yuán dàn
New Year's Day

春节
chūn jié
The lunar calendar New Year's Day

端午（端阳）
duān wǔ (duān yáng)
The Dragon Boat Festival

中秋
zhōng qiū

The Mid-Autumn Festival

圣诞节
shèng dàn jié
Christmas

阳历
yáng lì
solar calendar

阴历、农历
yīn lì, nóng lì
lunar calendar

月饼
yuè bǐn
moon cake

粽子
zòng zǐ
rice dumpling

B 汉译英
Translate the following sentences into English

[1] 端午节是阴历五月初五。在这一天我们要比赛划龙舟。
[2] 中秋节是农历八月十五, 这一天大家都要吃月饼。
[3] 粽子很好吃, 每年的端阳节我们都要吃粽子。
[4] 圣诞节快要到了, 我们太高兴了。
[5] 元旦和春节是中国人的两大节日, 每年人们都要过两个年。
[6] 一年有四季: 春、夏、秋、冬。
[7] 我喜欢冬天, 冬天可以滑雪, 夏天不能。
[8] 丽莎最喜欢秋天, 她说秋天的红叶最美丽。

[9] 一年要是有五个季就好了！
[10] 世界上有的地方一年只有两个季：旱季和雨季。

C 英译汉
Translate the following sentences into Chinese

[1] We celebrate two New Year's Days every year.

[2] Do you know which day of this year is the Mid-Autumn Day?

[3] What food do people eat on Dragon Festival Day?

[4] Christmas Day is always on Dec 25. However the Mid-Autumn Day is not on a fixed date on a solar calendar.

[5] We are so happy on Dragon Boat Festiva day. It is always May 5 on a lunar calendar; however it is not the same date on a solar calendar.

[6] Since winter is here already, spring must not be far away!

[7] On a winter day we went out to construct snow men. We played well in the cold weather.

[8] May I ask you which day is the Dragon-Boat Festival Day? Is it in May or in June?

[9] Uncle David will go to Australia to celebrate Christmas. However it is very hot on Christmas day there. Australia is cold in June and July.

[10] We sing songs on holidays and festival days, not only on our birthdays.

D 一首打油诗
A funny poem

春来不是读书天，
夏日炎炎正好眠；
秋有蚊虫冬寒冷，
背起书包等明年。

解释 Explanation

打油诗	dǎ yóu shī	funny poem
炎炎	yán yán	very hot
眠	mián	sleep
蚊虫	wén chóng	mosquitoes
书包	shū bāo	backpack
背起书包	bēi qǐ shū bāo	carry the backpack
等	děng	wait, wait for
明年	míng nián	the next year

(This funny poem came from a Chinese opera. In the play the lazy character refused to study hard. He claimed that no season was suitable for him to study.)

Lesson 9
The "Slow Motion"
第九课 走得慢的故事

小曼走路去看望就住在下一条街的老师，结果她第二年才走到老师的家。这是为什么呢？小曼是不是走得太慢了？

小曼的生日很奇怪，从上一次生日到这一次生日，不是过了一年，而是过了整整四年。这又是为什么呢？

小曼还有一件奇特的事：她刚从一个地方回来，那个地方居然没有北方，往随便哪个方向走都是朝南走。她真是"找不着北"了。

答案：

啊！小曼不是"小慢"。原来小曼是在 12 月 31 日晚上，一年的最后几分钟出发，走到老师家时自然已经跨入下一年,是下一年元旦的凌晨了。

小曼出生在闰年的2月29日,每4年才有一次2月有29天。

还有,小曼是去了北极。在那个地方往四方走都是向南,不可能更北了。

词汇 Words

看望	kàn wàng	visit
奇怪	qí guài	strange
生日	shēng rì	birthday
居然	jū rán	to one's surprise
随便	suí biàn	randomly
找不着北	zhǎo bù zháo běi	lost direction, no way
跨入	kuà rù	enter
元旦	yuán dàn	New Year's Day
凌晨	líng chén	early morning
闰年	rùn nián	leap year
北极	běi jí	The North Pole

练习 Exercise

这一课讲了3个问题:走得慢、生日、没有北。请你把课文译为英语。

This lesson talked about three problems: going too slow, strange birthday, and no north direction. Translate the whole text into English.

问题 Questions

[1] 闰年是怎么规定的？
How are leap years defined?

[2] 有没有一个地方没有南方，朝每个方向走都是向北？
Is there a place on Earth where every direction faces north?

[3] 有没有一个地方没有西方，朝每个方向走都是向东？
Is there a place on Earth where every direction faces the east?

实用汉语 Practical Chinese (9)
大学 University

A 词汇

系	xì	department
教授	jiào shòu	professor
实验室	shí yàn shì	lab
教室	jiào shì	classroom
副教授	fù jiào shòu	associate professor
助理教授	zhù lǐ jiào shòu	assistant professor
秘书	mì shū	secretary
科学家	kē xué jiā	scientist
物理学	wù lǐ xué	physics
化学	huà xué	chemistry
经济学	jīng jì xué	economics
法律	fǎ lǜ	law
校园	xiào yuán	campus
校长	xiào zhǎng	president
主任	zhǔ rèn	director
大学生	dà xué shēng	undergraduates
研究生	yān jiù shēng	graduate students
研究	yān jiù	research
资金	zī jīn	fund
有名的	yǒu míng de	famous

B 句型 Model sentences

[1] 这里是有名的西南大学。

[2] 这个楼是大学化学系，里面有很好的实验室。
[3] 我们大学有许多好教授，包括副教授和助理教授。
[4] 我们大学的校园真美丽！
[5] 王教授是这个系的系主任，有名的科学家。

C 用中、英文拟一份答问
Answer each question in both Chinese and English

[1] 这个大学的大学生多吗？
[2] 这里是哈佛(Harvard)大学吗？这个校园真美丽。
[3] 请问你是法律系的学生吗？
[4] 经济系的海德教授还需要研究生吗？我想申请。
[5] 对不起，资金没有了。你还有什么别的问题吗？

D 把下面的一段话译为汉语（口述答案，如果能写出更好）
Translate the following paragraph into Chinese. Read your answer and (if you can) write your answer in Chinese.

James is an American. He studies physics at the University of Pittsburgh. Last year he went to China to study physics there. In Peking University James read many books, went to the physics lab and did research work. James loved the beautiful campus of Peking University. He was told that the campus was the campus of Yanching University more than 60 years ago. The president of Yanching University was Mr. John Leighton Stuart, a great American. He helped many Chinese students.

词汇 Words

匹兹堡
Pí zī bǎo
Pittsburgh

北京大学
Běi jīng dà xué
Peking (Beijing) University

燕京大学
Yān jīng dà xué
Yanching University

司徒雷登
Sī tú léi dēng
Mr. John Leighton Stuart

匹兹堡大学 The Cathedral of Learning, University of Pittsburgh

Lesson 10
True or False?
第十课 大实话

以下几句话是"大实话"吗?

[1] 同样体积的液体没有钢铁重。
[2] 1月份比7月份要冷。
[3] 所有东西都是热胀冷缩。
[4] 没有摩擦车辆会行驶得更快。
[5] 不断地加热,温度会不断上升。

[答案] 都不是大实话。
　[1] 同样体积的水银(汞)就比钢铁重,如果到了太空所有的重力都消失了。
　[2] 在北半球对,但是在南半球(例如澳大利亚),7月比1月更冷。
　[3] 水在0摄氏度到4摄氏度之间是热缩冷胀。正因为如此,4摄氏度的水比重才最大。北方的湖冬季水面结了冰,但湖底仍然是水,鱼类才不致于死亡。

[4] 没有摩擦车辆根本不能起步，一步也行不了。已经在滑行的车辆也停不下来。

[5] 把冰加热直到变成水蒸气，温度不是一直上升的，是上升、停止、再上升、再停止，再上升的。水在在0摄氏度和100摄氏度会发生相变，那时温度会停止不动直到相变完全完成。所有晶体物质都有固定的熔点和汽化温度。

词汇 Words

大实话	dà shí huà	plain truth, always true
体积	tǐ jí	volume
液体	yè tǐ	liquid
钢铁	gāng tiě	steel, iron
摩擦	mō cā	friction
车辆	chē liǎng	vehicle
温度	wēn dù	temperature
水银（汞）	shuǐ yín (gǒng)	mercury
太空	tài kōng	outer space
南半球	nán bàn qiú	Southern Hemisphere
北半球	běi bàn qiú	Northern Hemisphere
澳大利亚	ào dà lì yà	Australia
摄氏度	shè shì dù	degree Celsius
华氏度	huá shì dù	degree Fahrenheit
起步	qǐ bù	start the motion
滑行	huá xíng	slide
水蒸气	shuǐ zhēng qì	water vapor, steam
相变	xiàng biàn	phase change
晶体	jīng tǐ	crystal

物质	wù zhì	material
熔点	róng diǎn	melting point
汽化	qì huà	vaporization

成语 Idiom
热胀冷缩　　rè zhàng lěng suō　　thermal expansion
(Volume or length increases when heated, decreases when cooled)

实用汉语 Practical Chinese (10)
知识 Knowledge:
温度及其它
Temperatures and more

[1] 摄氏温度和华氏温度的关系
Relation between degree Fahrenheit and degree Celsius.

水结冰是摄氏 0 度（华氏 32 度），人的体温接近华氏 100 度（华氏 100 度 = 摄氏 37.8 度）。在地面高度，水沸腾是摄氏 100 度（华氏 212 度）。

Water freezes at 0 °C (32 degrees Fahrenheit). Human body normal temperature is close to $100°F$ ($100°F=37.8°C$). On the ground water boils at $100°C$ (which is equal to $212°F$).

要把华氏温度换算成摄氏温度，只需先减去 32 度，再乘以 5，除以 9。

要把摄氏温度换算成华氏温度，只需乘以 9，除以 5，再加上 32 度。

To exchange between degree Fahrenheit and degree Celsius:
$$C = \frac{5}{9}(F-32) \qquad F = \frac{9}{5}C + 32,$$

例：摄氏 20 度等于华氏多少度？

Example: convert 20 degree Celsius to degree Fahrenheit.
$$F = \frac{9}{5}C + 32 = \frac{9}{5} \times 20 + 32 = 68°F$$

例：华氏 20 度等于摄氏多少度？
Example: convert 20 degree Fahrenheit to degree Celsius.
$$C = \frac{5}{9}(F - 32) = \frac{5}{9}(20 - 32) \approx -6.7°C$$

[2] 质量和重量的关系
Relation between mass and weight

质量是常数与地点无关，重量与在地球的什么地方有关。在太空物体质量不变而重量消失。

质量是标量没有方向，重量是矢量有方向。它们的单位不同。

Relation between mass and weight: Mass is a constant, weight depends on the location on Earth. In outer space objects are weightless, but still have the same mass.

Mass is a scalar without direction, weight is a vector and has its direction. They have different units.

练习 Exercises

[1] 除了澳大利亚以外，再举出 1 个 1 月比 7 月更热的国家的例子。

Give an example other than Australia where the weather is warmer in January than in July.

[2] 写 1 篇短文：想象一个没有摩擦力的世界。

Write a short article in Chinese: "Imagine a frictionless world".

[3] 定性地画出图，表现不断加热时零下10度的冰变成120度的水蒸气的温度变化过程。

Heat a piece of $-10°C$ ice until it becomes $120°C$ steam, sketch a diagram to show the change of temperature.

[4] 计算：摄氏30度等于华氏多少度？
Find how many degrees Fahrenheit is 30 degrees Celsius.

[5] 计算：华氏70度等于摄氏多少度？
Find how many degrees Celsius is 70 degrees Fahrenheit.

[6] 计算：摄氏温度数值正好等于华氏温度时，温度是多少度？
At what temperature is the reading the same in Fahrenheit scale and in Celsius scale?

[7] 课文里为什么说"在地面高度，水沸腾是摄氏100度（华氏212度）"，如果在高山上会有什么不同？
The text told us that "on the ground water boils at $100°C$ (which is equal to $212°F$)". What would happen if it is not on the ground, instead on the top of a high mountain?

(第[6]题答案：零下40度)
(Answer of question [6]: minus 40 degrees)
$$-40°C = -40°F$$

Lesson 11
Rules to Make a Turn
第十一课 转弯的学问

温迪老师问大家：如果从家到学校，要向右转一次，那么从学校沿来路回家应该怎么转弯？该变成向左转还是该不变仍然向右转呢？

大家说：当然是要反过来啦，变成向左转。右转变成左转。

温迪老师表扬大家说得对。接下来她又问大家：如果从家到学校要转两次，先向左转再向右转；那么当你沿来路从学校回家时，应该怎么办？是仍然先向左转然后再向右转，还是变成先向右转再向左转呢？

皮特说：还是先左转再右转。斯提文说：该反过来，变成先右转再左转。你认为他们谁是正确的呢？

词汇 Words

转弯	zhuǎn wān	make a turn
学问	xué wèn	knowledge
左（右）转	zuǒ (yòu) zhuǎn	left (right) turn
表扬	biǎo yáng	praise
仍然	réng rán	still
正确	zhèng què	correct

问题 Questions

[1] 斯提文和皮特，谁说得对？为什么？（请你看下图就知道答案了）。这个答案是不是有点出乎你的意料？

Who was right, Peter or Steven? Why? (Consider the following diagram). Are you surprised?

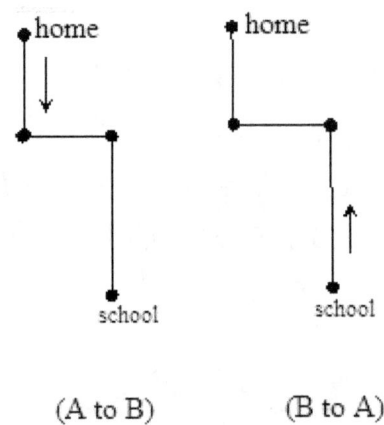

(A to B)　　(B to A)

[2] 如果你还不懂其中的道理，请你画图并和老师讨论。如果你已经明白道理，请回答：小索非亚从家到学校要一连转

6次弯：依顺序是右左左右左右，请问当她沿原路从学校返家时，该怎么转弯？

If you don't see why, discuss it with your teacher.

If you understand the theory, please answer the following question:

"When little Sophia goes from home to her school she needs to make six turns in order of RLLRLR. When she returns home from her school, what would be the order of turns?"

（答案：[1] 皮特对。[2] 左右左右右左）

实用汉语 Practical Chinese (11)
指路 Getting directions

课文：Text

这座城市有很多人，城市的面貌在不停地改变。一条条新的街道、一座座新立交桥每个月都在出现，一幢幢高楼像春笋一样拔地而起。不要说爷爷奶奶，就是我们年轻人也经常迷路，"找不着北"。

This city has many people; its appearance is changing everyday

邻居大爷看在眼里、疼在心里。他不顾年纪老迈，每天站在不同的道路边仔细观察。功夫不负有心人，他终于画出了一幅当地的最新地图，印了很多份。大爷的地图不仅表明哪里有超市、哪里有商场，还专门标出了路上卫生间的位置，方便群众。

行人要问爷爷买地图,他总是笑一笑,白送一张给那行人。他说:我作这事不是为了钱,而是为了让大家的生活容易些。

大家于是又忙碌地赶路。

词汇 Words

城市	chéng shì	city
面貌	miàn mào	looking, appearance
不停地	bù tíng dì	non-stop
改变	gǎi biàn	change
街道	jiē dào	street
立交桥	lì jiāo qiáo	overpass
一幢幢高楼	yī zhuàng zhàung gāo lóu	many buildings, one after another
春笋	chūn sǔn	spring bamboo shoot
找不着北	zhǎo bù zháo běi	lose direction
邻居	lín jū	neighbor
老迈	lǎo mài	old, hard to walk
仔细	zǐ xì	carefully
观察	guān chá	observe
超市	chāo shì	supermarket
商场	shāng chǎng	mall
卫生间(厕所)	wèi shēng jiān (cè suǒ)	restroom, washroom
地图	dì tú	map
群众	qún zhòng	people
忙碌	máng lù	busy
欢畅	huān chàng	happy

试试看你能不能不加帮助自己阅读下面这篇中文

Try to read and understand the following Chinese without help from others.

问路 Getting directions

汉语说"东南西北",也可以说"东西南北",但不说"西东北南"之类。

汉语里说"东北"、"西南",不说"北东"、"南西",与英语的说法 northeast,southwest 不同。

问路的时候,北京人会这样回答你"向西"、"向北";南方人往往告诉你"向左"、"向右"。这是因为,北京的街道大多是沿南北或者沿东西方向修建的,而很多南方城市不是这样。南方人到了北京,可能问路时还要加上一个在北京人看来是有趣的问题:"您告诉我朝东走,那么请问,哪个方向是东呢?"

我们说"买东西",不说"买南北"。但这"东西"并不是指东和西。

在中国,如果说"南方人"和"北方人",指的就是中国国内的南方各省的人和北方各省的人,但是如果说"西方人"和"东方人",就是指世界上西方国家的人和东方国家的人。中国人是东方人。

Lesson 12
Go Ahead of Time
第十二课 走在时间的前面

在万物中，光是走得最快的，在真空里光每秒钟跑30万千米。假使我们能飞行得比光速还快，就可以"追上"已经发出的光，看到过去发生过的事情。比方说100多年前流星撞上地球引起了一场大爆炸，那时的光早已向各方散去。但是如果我们的飞行速度超过光速，我们就能追上那一束光看见当年的大爆炸的火光。还可以先看到一个人死亡，再看见他的老年、中年、青少年，一直看到他倒变回到初生婴儿。

很遗憾那是不现实的。根据爱因斯坦的理论，一切速度都不能超过光速，人不能走在时间的前面。

然而，小姑娘雯雯却说：我有办法走在时间的前面，利用时差。比如4月15日星期五早上送一份传真从中国到美国，大洋对面的美国朋友收到电传的时间就是他们那里的4月14日星期四的晚上。你看，星期五送出、星期四就收到了，听起来不是很有意思吗？

这当然不是真的比时间走得更快，但是，老师和同学们还是称赞小雯雯特别聪明。

词汇 Words

真空	zhēn kōng	vacuum
千米	qiān mǐ	kilometer
假使	jiǎ shǐ	suppose, assume
流星	liú xīng	meteor
爆炸	bào zhà	explosion
死亡	sǐ wáng	death
婴儿	yīng ér	baby
遗憾	yí hàn	sorry, regret
爱因斯坦	ài yīn sī tǎn	Albert Einstein
理论	lǐ lùn	theory
时差	shí chā	time difference
传真、电传	chuán zhēn, diàn chuán	fax
称赞	chēng zàn	admire

问题 Questions

[1] 为什么星期五发出的电传，收到时是前一天即星期四呢？如果电传是由美国发给中国，能出现这样的情形吗？

How can one receive a fax on Thursday when the fax was sent out on Friday? If a fax is sent out from U.S.A to China, can that happen?

[2] 比较一下现代火箭的速度和光速，谁更快？差别大吗？

Compare the speed of modern rockets and the speed of light, which one is faster? Is the difference big?

练习 Exercise

在网上查找关于爱因斯坦的事，写 1 篇短文。

Read about Albert Einstein on the internet. Write a short article.

实用汉语 Practical Chinese (12)
朋友 Friends

A 词汇 Words

友谊	yǒu yí	friendship
真诚	zhēn chéng	sincere, true
宝贵	bǎo guì	valuable
鲜花	xiān huā	fresh flowers
生病	shēng bìng	sick
打电话	dǎ diàn huà	making a phone call
慰问	wèi wèn	express solicitude
看望	kàn wàng	visit
需要	xū yào	need
立刻	lì kè	immediately
交谈	jiāo tán	talk
帮助	bāng zhù	help
借钱	jiè qián	borrow money
解决问题	jiě jué wèn tí	solve problems
关心	guān xīn	concern
长久	cháng jiǔ	long time
城市	chéng shì	city
认识	rèn shì	know

B 句型 Model sentences

[1] 真诚的友谊是世界上最宝贵的。
Zhēn chéng de yuǒ yì shì shì jiè shàng zuì bǎo guì de.
Sincere friendship is the most valuable thing in the world.

[2] 朋友病了，我应该打电话慰问她或者送去鲜花。
Péng yǒu bìng le, wǒ yīng gāi dǎ diàn huà wèi wèn tā huó zhě sòng qù xiān huā.
A friend is sick. I should call her to express my concerns or visit her with flowers.

[3] 朋友向我借钱，我会热情相助，帮助他（她）度过难关。
Péng yǒu xiàng wǒ jiè qián, wǒ huì rè qíng xiāng zhù, bāng zhù tā (tā) dù guò nán guān.
If a friend needs to borrow money from me, I will lend money to her or him, help her or him pass the difficulty.

[4] 我经常看望朋友，和他们交谈。
Wǒ jīng cháng kàn wàng péng yǒu, hé tā men jiāo tán.
I often visit my friends and talk with them.

[5] 我愿意关心别人，别人也常常帮助我。我们都需要友谊。
Wǒ yuàn yì guān xīn bié rén, bié rén yě cháng cháng bāng zhù wǒ. Wǒ mén dōu xū yào yǒu yì.
I would like to help others. Others also help me. We all need friendship.

C 汉译英 Translate the following into English
[1] 汤姆和皮特都是我的朋友，我们常常一起学习。
[2] 艾米是张(zhang)的朋友，张是丽莎的朋友。
[3] 没有朋友的帮助我是不能够做好这件事的。
[4] 我要是能认识更多的朋友就太好了。
[5] 有一位朋友病了，我们都很关心她，立刻去看望她。

D 英译汉
Translate the following into Chinese

[1] Can you please tell my friend Tom that I would like to see him today?

[2] Where are your friends? Are they still around when you need them most?

[3] How many true friends do you have?

[4] My friend, may I borrow that book from you?

[5] Zhang has four good friends. One of them was sick today. Zhang went to visit her immediately.

Lesson 13
Story of the Sun and the Cold Wind
第十三课 太阳和秋风的故事

有个人在路上行走。

秋风和太阳打赌，看谁能让那个人把外衣脱掉。

秋风用劲地吹，想把那人的外衣吹掉。那人觉得凉风阵阵，就用手紧紧地抓住外衣不放。秋风失败了。

该太阳了，太阳把慈祥的阳光洒到世界上，那人觉得气温一点点地升起来，越来越温暖。终于，他觉得热了，自动地解开了纽扣，把外衣脱下来拿在手上。

太阳不如秋风厉害，但是太阳还是胜利了。

词汇 Words

寓言	yù yán	fable
打赌	dǎ dǔ	bet
外衣	wài yī	coat
纽扣	niǔ kòu	button
紧紧地抓住	jǐn jǐn dì zhuā zhù	grasp tightly
厉害	lì hài	powerful, terrible
失败	shī bài	fail
慈祥	cí xiáng	kindly

知识 Knowledge

寓言起源于民间，又经文人创作增添，短小的故事里充满智慧哲理，寓意深刻，东西方都有很多著名的寓言流传。

There are many famous fables all over the world. Fables tell readers important lessons from short stories.

问题 Questions

[1] 这篇寓言说明了什么道理？为什么秋风很厉害还是输了？

What lesson have you learned from this fable? Why did the cold wind lose the competition to the sun?

[2] 什么是寓言？寓言和童话、民间故事有什么区别？各举一例。

What are fables? What is the difference among a fable, a fairy tale, and a folk story? Give an example of each and study the difference.

实用汉语 Practical Chinese (13)
晚会 Party

A 口语练习

[1] 欢迎光临！
Huān yíng guāng lín !
Welcome!

[2] 请喝饮料。
Qǐng hē yǐn liào.
Please get something to drink.

[3] 请吃些蛋糕。
Qǐng chī xiē dàn gāo.
Please have some cake.

[4] 我可以问问您的名字吗？
Wǒ kě yǐ wèn wèn nín de míng zì mā?
May I ask you your name?

[5] 这位是史密斯先生，那位是华生夫人
Zhè wèi shì shǐ mì sī xiān shēng, nà wèi shì huá shēng fū rén.

This gentleman is Mr. Smith. That lady is Mrs. Watson.

[6] 这位是我的朋友汉娜。
Zhè wèi shì wǒ de péng yǒu hàn nā.
She is my friend Hanna.

[7] 那边有很多水果,请自己取用
Nà biān yǒu hěn duō shuǐ guǒ, qǐng zì jǐ qǔ yòng.
There are many kinds of fruits, please help yourself.

[8] 对不起,这里在开生日聚会,不能抽烟。
Duì bù qǐ, zhè lǐ zài kāi shēng rì jù huì, bú néng chōu yān.
Excuse me, here is a birthday party and is smoke free.

[9] 我们的聚会将在晚上9点结束。
Wǒ mén de jù huì jiāng zài wǎn shàng jiǔ diǎn jié shù.
Our party will end at 9 pm.

[10] 下次聚会该我们班主办了,欢迎大家都来。
Xià cì jù huì gāi wǒ mén bān zhǔ bàn le, huān yíng dà jiā dōu lái.
Next party will be hosted by our class. Everyone is welcome.

B 晚会上的常用词

酒、饮料、玻璃杯、炸薯片,炸薯条、
jiǔ, yǐn liào, bō lí bēi, zhà shǔ piàn, zhà shǔ tiáo
wine, beverage, glass, potato chips, French fries,

虾片、糖果、凉菜、三明治、咖啡、

xiā piàn, táng guǒ, liáng cài, sān míng zhì, kā fēi,
shrimp chips, candy, appetizer, sandwich, coffee,

热巧克力、椅子、凳子、桌子、红酒、
rè qiǎo kè lì, yǐ zǐ, dèng zǐ, zhuō zǐ, hóng jiǔ,
hot chocolate, chair, stool, table, red wine,

跳舞、唱歌、讲笑话、晚礼服、西装、
tiào wǔ, chàng gē, jiǎng xiào huà, wǎn lǐ fú, xī zhuāng,
dance, sing, comedy show, evening gown, suit,

欢迎再来、请、对不起、高兴、报幕、
huān yíng zài lái, qǐng, duì bú qǐ, gāo xìng, bào mù,
welcome back again, please, sorry, happy, announce,

放松、免费、唱戏、听音乐、弹钢琴、
fàng sōng, miǎn fèi, chàng xì, tīng yīn yuè, tán gāng qín,
relax, free, sing in an opera, listen to music, play a piano,

拉小提琴、照相、名片、认识、结识、
lā xiǎo tí qín, zhào xiàng, míng piàn, rèn shì, jié shí,
play a violin, taking photos, business card, meet, get to know,

感谢、主持人、节目单、漂亮、化装
gǎn xiè, zhǔ chí rén, jié mù dān, piào liàng, huà zhuāng
thank, host, play list, pretty, make up

C 用汉语设计答案回答问题
Design an answer for each question in Chinese.

[1] 今天的晚会几点开始？
[2] 有人知道晚会在哪里举行吗？
[3] 晚会真的很精彩 (wonderful)吗？
[4] 我可以带一个朋友参加晚会吗？
[5] 今天的晚会要买票吗？还是可以免费参加的？
[6] 我们的晚会准备有很多好的食品，您想来吗？
[7] 今天的晚会有京剧(Peking Opera)表演吗？
[8] 你的晚礼服太美了，我可以问问你是在哪里买的吗？
[9] 请问晚会上可以喝酒吗？我是个司机。
[10] 今天的晚会要开到什么时候结束？请问晚会结束后有跳舞吗？

Lesson 14
Monk *Tang* Crossed a River
第十四课 唐僧过河

这一天，前往西天取经的唐僧师徒四人来到了一条拦路河边。这条河很宽，对岸在远远的前方，河水也流得不慢，但是在已经经历千难万险的师徒眼里却比已经过了的凶险无比、浊浪翻天的好几条大河要平静得多了。河边没有渡船也没有人影。大徒弟孙悟空让师父先在岸边休息一下，自己腾云到前边去探一下情况。

猪八戒不肯听话，劝师父说："师父，这条河看起来一点儿也不深，您就是淌水也走得过去。不信咱们找土地老儿来问问"。

他当真把土地老儿找来了。八戒问道："土地，你知道这河的深度吗？"，土地老连忙回答："这条河的平均深度只有2尺"。八戒听了，哈哈大笑："师父，您听见了吧。快别等那猴哥了。咱们走吧，2尺深就是不骑马，师父您从河水里淌也淌过去了"。唐僧和沙和尚也觉得这么过河可以。

便在此时黄影一闪,孙悟空飞了回来,大喊:"且慢!"

三人赶紧问:"是水里有食人鱼吗?"

"非也",孙悟空说道,"我已查明,此河里并没有食人鱼,也没有妖怪。河水的平均深度的确也只有2尺,不过,师父还是淌不过去的。"

你们知道孙悟空为什么那样做吗?八戒说的不是听起来有道理吗?请大家想一想答案。"

经过热烈讨论,大家明白了八戒所说其实是似是而非的。因为土地老儿只说了河水的平均深度,并没有说最深的地方有多深。平均2尺深,最深的地方完全可能远远超过2尺甚至7、8尺,令唐僧即使骑马也不能过去,更不要说淌水了。悟空师兄弟虽然有本事腾云驾雾,却背不动凡人的唐僧(否则西天取经就不必费时费事了)。

从这个故事看来，虽然平均值用的很广，有的时候最大或最小值却可能起决定作用。一堆产品不能只是平均量合格，需要长2米的钢条，你就不能给人家长长短短的一堆钢条说它们的平均长度是2米。

背景解释 The background

"西游记"是中国著名的长篇小说，为明朝吴承恩所著。小说以唐代玄奘和尚到印度取经的事实为基础加以文学加工，描写了唐僧及其徒弟孙悟空、猪八戒、沙僧，克服万难，战胜妖魔和凶险，胜利到达西天取得真经的故事。这篇课文不是西游记里的，仅仅是借唐僧师徒取经的背景写成的。

"Journey to the West" is a famous long novel in China, written by Wu Cheng En (1499 – 1582). The novel was based on the fact that monk Xuan Zhuang (602 – 664) of Tang Dynasty traveled to India to study Buddhism. In the novel Master Monk Tang, his chief assistant Sun Wu Kong (the Monkey King), other assistants Zhu Ba Jie (the great pig), Sha Seng (a former monster), together fought many enemies and completed the dangerous long journey to India. This story is not a part of the original book but merely uses the book as the background.

词汇 Words

西天	xī tiān	The western world (here it means India)
取经	qǔ jīng	learn Buddhism
唐僧师徒	táng sēng shī tú	(see the above explanation)

拦路	lán lù	block the way
经历	jīng lì	undergo through
凶险	xiōng xiǎn	danger
无比	wú bǐ	nothing similar
浊浪	zhuó làng	dirty water waves
翻天	fān tiān	rush towards the sky
平静	píng jìng	calm
腾云	téng yún	ride the clouds, fly in the sky
渡船	dù chuán	ferry boat
趟水	tàng shuǐ	walk through the river
且慢	qiě màn	wait a minute
土地老儿	tǔ dì lǎo ér	the local officer in legend
食人鱼	shí rén yú	piranha
平均深度	píng jūn shēn dù	the average depth
热烈讨论	rè liè tǎo lùn	warm discussion
最深	zuì shēn	the deepest
最大值	zuì dà zhí	the maximum
长	cháng	long, length
凡人	fán rén	ordinary people
短	duǎn	short
最小值	zuì xiǎo zhí	the minimum
非也	fēi yě	no

成语 Idioms

千难万险
qiān nán wàn xiǎn
numerous difficulties

浊浪翻天
zhuó làng fān tiān
dirty waves shake, rush towards the sky

腾云驾雾
téng yún jià wù
ride the clouds, fly over the mist

问题 Question

在唐僧过河这个故事里，重要的是河水的最大深度。你能想出个最小值起决定作用的例子吗？

In this story the maximum value of the depth of the river made the biggest difference. Can you think about a situation where the minimum value would make a big difference in deciding the final result?

实用汉语 Practical Chinese (14)
旅行 Travel

旅行者　　A traveller in Death Valley National Park, USA

对话 Dialogue
------ 你准备去旅行吗？
------ 是的，明天就出发。
------ 去哪里旅行呢？
------ 去中国的黄山。
------ 你一个人去吗？
------ 不，我跟旅游团去，我们一共有30多个人。
------ 那很好呀，你了解中国吗？
------ 诚实地说，了解得还不多。
------ 没关系，导游会讲给你听的。
------ 比如我不知道，除了黄山以外中国还有没有旅游地点叫"绿山"或者"红山"。
------ 啊，有趣的问题。

------ 我知道这本书的作者 Betz 老师和常博士还写了下一本书，叫做"高级汉语------了解中国"。
------ 是的。你准备继续学习这下一本书吗？
------ 当然。学习之后我会对中国了解得更多的。
------ 那好，让我们一起学习吧。

词汇 Words

旅行	lǚ xíng	travel
黄山	huáng shān	The Yellow Mountains
旅游团	lǚ yóu tuán	tourist group
导游	dào yóu	tourist guide
有趣	yǒu qù	interesting
继续	jì xù	continue

汉译英
Translate the following into English

[1] 我要参加旅游团去英国旅游，很有趣呢！

[2] 去旅行要带上护照(passport)，钱和地图。

[3] 你喜欢旅行吗？是的，我非常喜欢，我每年都要旅行。

[4] 我每年都要旅行两次。今年去中国的桂林(Guilin)和澳大利亚的悉尼(Sidney, Australia).

[5] 你去西藏(Tibet)旅行吗？我想去，但是不知道身体能不能行，旅行虽然有趣但也很辛苦。

[6] 在汉语里我们说东南西北或者东西南北，但不说北西南东。

[7] 我们说"买东西"，不说"买南北"。但这"东西"并不是指东和西。

英译汉

Translate the following into Chinese

[1] Travel is very good for us. Travel makes us healthy and happy.

[2] I want to travel but I do not have enough money.

[3] Can I travel with you to Tibet? I want to go there.

[4] Our tourist guide book is very good. I need it when I go to China.

[5] You said you would go to London（伦敦）, Canada, but actually you went to London, England.

Lesson 15
Are Scientists Wrong?
第十五课 科学家错了吗？

维克多的爸爸是一位科学家，他跟随南极考察远洋船队去南极作科学考察，离开家已经几个月了。

这天维克多收到了爸爸远道寄来的信。维克多高兴极了，马上拆开来读。爸爸在信上说："我们先到了磁北极，接着又来到一个地方，这里没有南方，24小时都是白天。"

维克多不明白了，是爸爸错了吗？明明是去南极为什么会到了"北极"呢？既然是向南去，怎么会说没有南呢？还有，白天之后是夜晚，怎么会24小时都是白天呢？

琳达老师告诉维克多，地球是一个大的天然磁铁。只是磁北极在地理南极的旁边，磁南极在地理北极的旁边。所以一个小磁铁的南极受到地球磁北极的吸引才会指向地理的南方。还有，走到了地理南极，就不可能再向南了。

从地理南极朝任何一个方向走都是向北。南极地区半年都是白天，下一个半年就全是黑夜。

维克多明白了这些关于南极的知识，他立志长大后要像爸爸一样，当个科学家去南极或者北极作科学考察。

词汇 Words

科学	kē xué	science
科学家	kē xué jiā	scientist
远道	yuǎn dào	far away
考察	kǎo chá	expedition
磁北极	cí běi jí	magnetic North Pole
磁南极	cí nán jí	magnetic South Pole
地球	dì qiú	Earth
天然磁体	tiān rán cí tǐ	natural magnet
地理南极	dì lǐ nán jí	geographic South Pole
地理北极	dì lǐ běi jí	geographic North Pole
南极地区	nán jí dì qū	Antarctic region

问题 Questions

[1] 如果维克多的爸爸是到北极考察，那封信会怎样写呢？

Assume Victor's dad went to the North Pole instead of the Antarctic region, what would the letter say in that case?

[2] 有没有一个地点叫西极，往任何方向走都是向东呢？

Is there a place "West Pole", where every direction is pointing towards the east?

[3] 为什么指南针会指向南方呢？

Why does a compass always point to the direction of south?

Jamie dreams of becoming a fighter jet pilot.
杰米的理想是做一个战斗机飞行员，飞翔在蓝天。

实用汉语 Practical Chinese (15)
理想 Dreams（1）

A. 单词 Words

理想	lǐ xiǎng	dream
生物	shēng wù	living creatures
基因	jī yīn	gene
人类	rén lèi	mankind, human
贡献	gòng xiàn	contribution
战斗机	zhàn dòu jī	fighter jet
飞行员	fēi xíng yuán	pilot
飞翔	fēi xiáng	fly
蓝天	lán tiān	blue sky
政治家	zhèng zhì jiā	politician
领导人	lǐng dào rén	leader
文学家	wén xué jiā	writer
惊人	jīng rén	amazing
作品	zuò pǐn	work

B. 课文 Text

丹丹的理想是长大后成为一个科学家，研究生物的基因，为人们的生活做出贡献。杰米的理想是做一个战斗机飞行员，飞翔在蓝天。理查德的理想是做一个政治家，将来成为国家的领导人。埃米的理想是当一个文学家，写出惊人的作品。

Dān dān de lǐ xiǎng shì zhǎng dà hòu chéng wéi yī gè kē xué jiā, yān jiù shēng wù de jī yīn, wèi rén mén de shēng huó zuò chū gòng xiàn. Jié mǐ de lǐ xiǎng shì zuò yī gè zhàn dòu jī fēi xíng yuán, fēi xiáng zài lán tiān. Lǐ chá dé de lǐ xiǎng shì zuò yī gè zhèng zhì jiā, jiāng lái chéng wéi guó jiā de lǐng dào rén. Ai mǐ de lǐ xiǎng shì dāng yī gè wén xué jiā, xiě chū jīng rén de zuò pǐn.

The dream of Dan Dan is to grow up and become a scientist, study genes and make a contribution to human life. Jamie dreams of becoming a fighter jet pilot and fly freely in the blue sky. Richard wants to become a politician and be the leader of the country someday. Amy dreams of becoming a writer, producing amazing works of literature.

C.
你少年时的理想是什么？
写一篇中文的短文讲述自己少年时期的梦。
Write an article in Chinese to tell people what your dream was when you were a child.

Lesson 16
Confucius and Two Kids
第十六课 孔子和两个小儿的故事

有一天，孔子看见两个小儿在争论。

小儿甲说：太阳早上离我们近。因为早上的太阳看起来比中午的太阳大。越近看起来就会越大。

小儿乙说：太阳中午离我们近。因为中午比早上热。太阳离我们越近，我们应该感觉越热。

孔子是我国古代的大思想家、教育家。他教育学生不要单纯读书，而要学习"六艺"，包括射箭、音乐等。然而这一次孔子也不知道该怎么回答。他就坦然承认自己不懂。

孔子的这个态度，就是他说过的"知之为知之，不知为不知，是知也"。是很诚实的为人之道和治学态度。

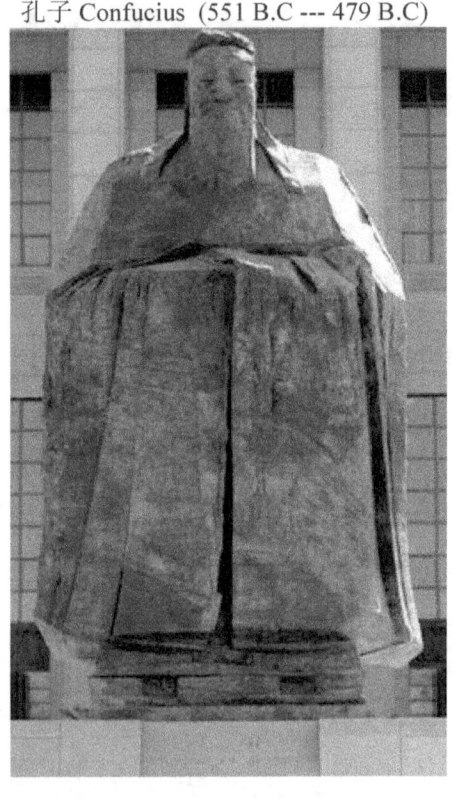

孔子 Confucius (551 B.C --- 479 B.C)

词汇 Words

争论	zhēng lùn	debate
坦然	tǎn rán	calm, frank
思想家	sī xiǎng jiā	thinker
教育家	jiào yù jiā	educator

单纯	dān chún	simple, pure
射箭	shè jiàn	archery
音乐	yīn yuè	music
然而	rán ér	however
坦然	tǎn rán	frankly, calm
承认	chéng rèn	admit
态度	tài dù	attitude
诚实	chéng shí	honest
用人之道	yòng rén zhī dào	the way to treat and manage people
治学	zhì xué	study, scholarship

问题 Question

什么是"知之为知之，不知为不知，是知也"？为什么说这是聪明的态度？

"If you know, say you know; if you don't know, admit that you don't know". Why is such an attitude wise?

练习 Exercises

[1] 在网上学习有关天文的知识，试图去给出一个正确的答案。

Learn about astronomy online and find your answer to the debate of the kids.

[2] "吾日三省吾身"，检查一下自己是否做到了"知之为知之，不知为不知"。

"Examine myself three times a day", see whether you have reached the wise state of "if you know, say you know; if you don't know, admit that you don't know".

实用汉语 Practical Chinese (16)
理想 Dreams（2）

A. 单词 Words

画家	huà jiā	artist
到达	dào dá	reach
艺术	yì shù	art
高峰	gāo fēng	summit, peak
医生	yī shēng	doctor
探险家	tàn xiǎn jiā	explorer
运动员	yùn dòng yuán	athlete
教师	jiào shī	teacher
记者	jì zhě	correspondent
企业家	qǐ yè jiā	entrepreneurs
杰出	jié chū	extraordinary
企业	qǐ yè	business

B. 课文 Text

伊丽莎白的理想是成为一个画家，画出最美的图画，攀登艺术的高峰。班里其他同学也有各自的理想，有的想当医生、探险家，有的想当运动员，有的想做教师或者记者。还有一人梦想成为一个杰出的企业家，建立一个大企业。

Yī lì shā bái de lǐ xiǎng shì chéng wéi yī gè huà jiā, huà chū zuì měi de tú huà, pān dēng yì shù de gāo fēng. Bān lǐ qí tā de tóng xué yě yǒu gè zì de lǐ xiǎng, yǒu dé xiǎng dāng yī sheng, tàn xiǎn jiā, yǒu dé xiǎng dāng yùn dòng yuán, yǒu dé xiǎng zuò jiào shī huò zhě jì zhě. Hái yǒu yī rén mèng xiǎng chéng wéi yī gè jié chū de qì yè jiā, jiàn lì yī gè dà qì yè.

  Elizabeth's dream is to become an artist in the future, creating the most beautiful paintings to reach the summit of arts. Other students of the class also have their dreams. Some students want to become doctors, explorers, athletes, teachers, or journalists. One student wants to become a great entrepreneur and lay the foundation to a big business.

C.
你现在的理想是什么？
怎样才能实现自己的梦想？
Write an article in Chinese about your dream.
  What do you need to do now, in order to let your dream become true in the future?

www.ingramcontent.com/pod-product-compliance
Lightning Source LLC
Chambersburg PA
CBHW061420300426
44114CB00015B/2005